Love & Light Meditation

Written by Carol Ann Lacina

Illustrated by Zachery Manza Wideman

All rights reserved. © 2019 Carol Ann Lacina

*"To my three children,
Danielle, Cassandra, and John
who have shown me the beauty of love;
and to all the children in the world
who may need more of it."*

Text and Illustrations:
Copyright © 2019, Carol Ann Lacina
All rights reserved.
www.carolannlacina.com

Illustrations, cover design and page layout:
Zachery Manza Wideman
www.widemanillustrations.com

No part of this book may be reproduced,
copied or transmitted without
the written permission of the author.

All rights reserved. © Carol Ann Lacina 2019

Sit up straight with your legs crossed, your hands on your knees, and your palms facing upward towards the sky.

Now close your eyes and take a deep breath,

in through your nose,

and then release your breath through your mouth.

Pretend there is a cord coming from the base of your spine, that extends deep into the earth.

Imagine the inside of the earth is beautiful, magical,

with gorgeous crystals and light shining from everywhere.

Pretend your cord is spiraling deep into the center of the earth and wrap it around the center.

Pretend there is an intense light beaming from the earth.

Bring that beautiful, loving light up from the earth, and into your body through your spine.

Your body is filling up with this light,

each and every body part is filling up with the light, and the love it brings.

The light is now pouring out from the top of your head, and from your heart.
Imagine this loving light is white and iridescent, and imagine it sprinkling all over you and around your body.

This light is filled with love and will comfort and bless you.

Now open your eyes.

Imagine this light can expand outwards,

and you can touch others with this light.

Imagine this light is coming out of your hands and heart, or you have a beautiful wand in your hand, and you can sprinkle this light on anyone you want.

When you go out for the day you can bless others with this light, this light of love, and sprinkle this light on anyone or everyone you meet.

You can sprinkle this light on someone you love if they are sad or angry.

It will cheer them up, and help to calm them down.

This light is so strong that by sending them light, they will feel better, and will be able to feel the light and love you are sending them immediately!

So, enjoy this light within you,

spreading within your body,

expanding out to others

to help heal the world

from their pain and sadness too!

As you truly are a beautiful being of light!

Carol Ann was born and raised in New Jersey, along with her six brothers, where she currently resides, and is the Mother of three beautiful souls. She has always had a passion for writing, starting her first journal in Elementary School, and always found comfort in her writing. She is a Certified Reiki Practitioner, and has educated people about Reiki and energy healing through her articles in Natural Awakenings Magazine, her websites, blogs, and social media accounts. Carol Ann has been caring for young children since High School, and loves their energy, joy, and innocence. She has helped in caring for her 22 nieces and nephews, and has 13 great nieces and nephews that she loves and adores dearly! Her love for children and writing is a perfect combination to create books for children. Carol Ann believes by helping the children focus on love, brings the comfort they may need on their journey ahead through life.

Made in the USA
Lexington, KY
08 November 2019